KB244459

A Gallery of Ghosts

About Wise & Wide

- A systematic 6-level English reading program based on Lexile® measures
- Diverse and interesting topics chosen from the elementary curriculums of Korea and English speaking western countries
- Well-written books in various forms including fiction stories, descriptive texts, and classics retold
- The informative but original fiction stories grab your interest, leading to the easy and clear understanding of the educational content.
- Improve thinking skills with solid after-reading activities at all levels of the series.

Wise & Wide is a 6-level English reading program that consists of 60 books and each level is systematically divided by Lexile® measures. The Lexile® Framework for Reading is the most popular reading measuring system in American formal education curriculums and many English programs. Over 20 out of 50 states in the U.S. mark Lexile® measures directly on students' final report cards and over 300 well-known publishers adopt and use Lexile® measures.

Experience many kinds of readings written by professional writers from the U.S. and England. They used interesting topics that were carefully chosen after analyzing elementary curriculums from around the world including Korea, the U.S., England, and Australia among many others. Comprehensive after-reading activities including graphic organizers, speaking tasks, and After-reading Tests are ready for you.

Levels in the series and their corresponding Lexile® measures

Level	Lexile® measures	U.S. Grade
Level 1	Below 200L	Pre K - K
Level 2	190L - 400L	Lower Grade 1
Level 3	350L - 530L	Upper Grade 1
Level 4	420L - 650L	Grade 2
Level 5	520L - 940L	Grade 3 - 4
Level 6	830L - 1070L	Grade 5 - 6

* Smart Readers: Wise & Wide level 1 is applicable to the preschool level in the U.S.

* The source of the relationship between Lexile® measures and U.S. school grades: CCSS(Common Core State Standards) FOR ENGLISH LANGUAGE ARTS, APPENDIX A (2012, which is used by 45 states in the U.S.)

Topic List

	Level 1	Level 2	Level 3	Level 4	Level 5	Level 6
Book 1	Science〉Biology: The hibernation of animals Story	Science〉Biology: Living and nonliving things Story	Science〉Biology〉 Animals & the Environment: Sea otters Story	Environment〉 Living with nature: The diver & the persimmon tree Story	Science〉Biology〉 Animal: Amazing animals of the Amazon Story	Science〉Biology: Germs, transmitted diseases Story
Book 2	Literature〉 World classics: Aesop's fables Story	Literature〉 Traditional fairy tale: Old tales about stones Story	Social Studies〉 Economy: To run a business to make and save money Story	Science〉Biology〉 Plants: Photosynthesis Story	Science〉Earth science: Earth's layers,earthquakes, volcanoes, and earth's atmosphere Report	Mathematics〉 Sequence: The golden ratio & the Fibonacci sequence Story
Book 3	Science〉Physics: How shadows are formed Story	Literature〉 World classics: Peter Pan Story	Science〉Scientific technology: Nanobots Story	Literature〉Myths: World's creation stories Story	Literature〉 Legend: The story of King Arthur Story	Literature〉Myths: Constellation myths Story
Book 4	Literature〉 Traditional literature: The Talmud Story	Science〉Biology〉 Animal: Polar bears Story	Science〉Biology〉 Animal: Mountain gorillas Story	Social Studies〉 Cultural anthropology: Amazing ancient cultures of the world Story	Science〉 Earth science: Clouds and weather Story	Literature〉 Human and animals: The friendship between a girl & a horse Story
Book 5	Social Studies〉 Ethics: Rules in daily life Story	Science〉Biology : The five senses Report	Social Studies〉 Cultural anthropology: Astonishing festivals Report	Art〉Music: Stories from two operas Story	Social Studies〉 World culture & history: The Renaissance Story	
Book 6	Social Studies〉 World geography & travel: Tourist attractions around the world Story	Science〉Biology〉 Animal: Dinosaurs Story	Science〉 Astronomy: The solar system Story	Social Studies〉 People: Three great people who overcame hardships Story	Science〉Scientific technology: The wonderful world of robots Report	
Book 7		Social Studies〉 Cultural anthropology: Mythological monsters from around the world Report		Science & Social Studies〉 Technology & culture: Inventions from around the world Report	Art〉Works of art: Famous paintings Report	
Book 8				Social Studies〉 History: the California Gold Rush Report	Social Studies & Science〉 Psychology: Psychology in everyday life Story	
Book 9						
Book 10						

* 10 books in each level will be published.

How to Use This Book

•Before Reading

You can easily find the topic and what kind of story you are about to read.

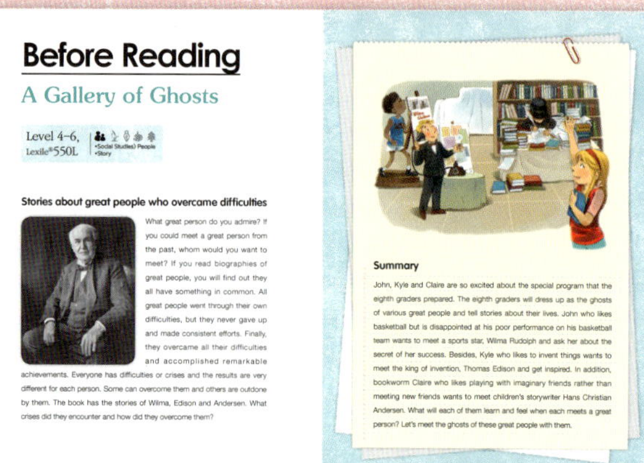

•The text

All the stories were written by professional writers from the U.S. and England, so you will read authentic and appropriate English sentences and expressions in every book in the series.

•Pop Quiz

Check out right away if you understand what you have just read by solving a pop quiz that checks your comprehension.

•Key Words

The key words and expressions on each page are listed for you to easily study them.

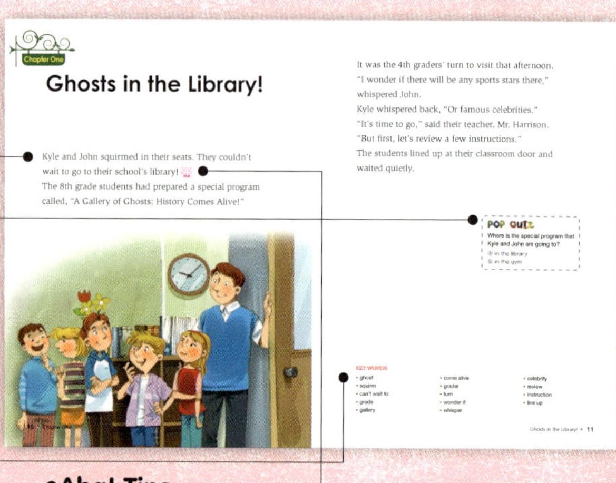

•Aha! Tips

Download free Korean explanations at *www.ihappyhouse.co.kr* for all of the sentences marked with "Aha!". These explain cultural, scientific, and economic knowledge or they deal with aspects of English such as grammatical structures or idiomatic expressions. There are lots of "Aha! Tips" to help you understand the text.

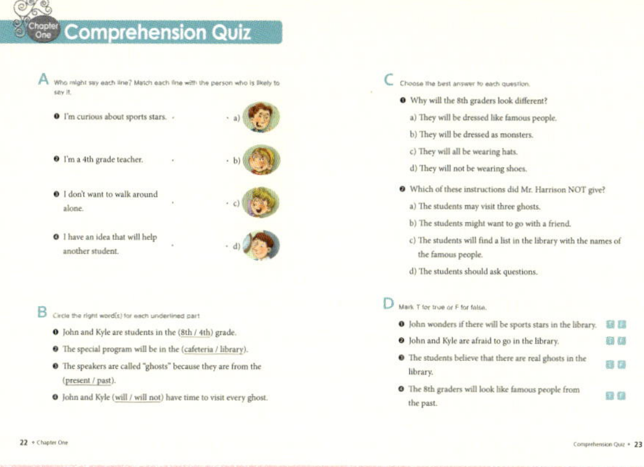

•Comprehension Quiz

After reading one chapter, solve various questions to find out if you fully understand the content.

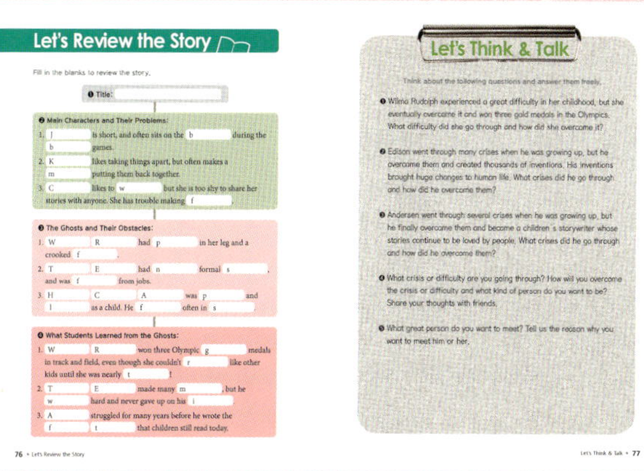

•Let's Review the Story /
•Let's Think & Talk

Fill in the blanks in the organizer to summarize the whole story. Express your own thinking and feelings about the story by answering the questions. You can build up logic and reasoning skills for your essay examinations in the future.

Appendix

Audio CD

In the CD audio book form, the texts are read vividly by American professional voice actors.

After-reading Test

Solve an additionally provided After-reading Test for each book.

The Korean translation, Answer Keys, a Word Quiz, a Word List, and Aha! Tips for each book

You can download them for free at *www.ihappyhouse.co.kr*

Before Reading

A Gallery of Ghosts

Level 4-6,
Lexile®550L

•Social Studies〉People
•Story

Stories about great people who overcame difficulties

What great person do you admire? If you could meet a great person from the past, whom would you want to meet? If you read biographies of great people, you will find out they all have something in common. All great people went through their own difficulties, but they never gave up and made consistent efforts. Finally, they overcame all their difficulties and accomplished remarkable achievements. Everyone has difficulties or crises and the results are very different for each person. Some can overcome them and others are outdone by them. The book has the stories of Wilma, Edison and Andersen. What crises did they encounter and how did they overcome them?

Summary

John, Kyle and Claire are so excited about the special program that the eighth graders prepared. The eighth graders will dress up as the ghosts of various great people and tell stories about their lives. John who likes basketball but is disappointed at his poor performance on his basketball team wants to meet a sports star, Wilma Rudolph and ask her about the secret of her success. Besides, Kyle who likes to invent things wants to meet the king of invention, Thomas Edison and get inspired. In addition, bookworm Claire who likes playing with imaginary friends rather than meeting new friends wants to meet children's storywriter Hans Christian Andersen. What will each of them learn and feel when each meets a great person? Let's meet the ghosts of these great people with them.

Contents

A Gallery of Ghosts

A Gallery of Ghosts

Chapter One

Ghosts in the Library!

Kyle and John squirmed in their seats. They couldn't wait to go to their school's library!

The 8th grade students had prepared a special program called, "A Gallery of Ghosts: History Comes Alive!"

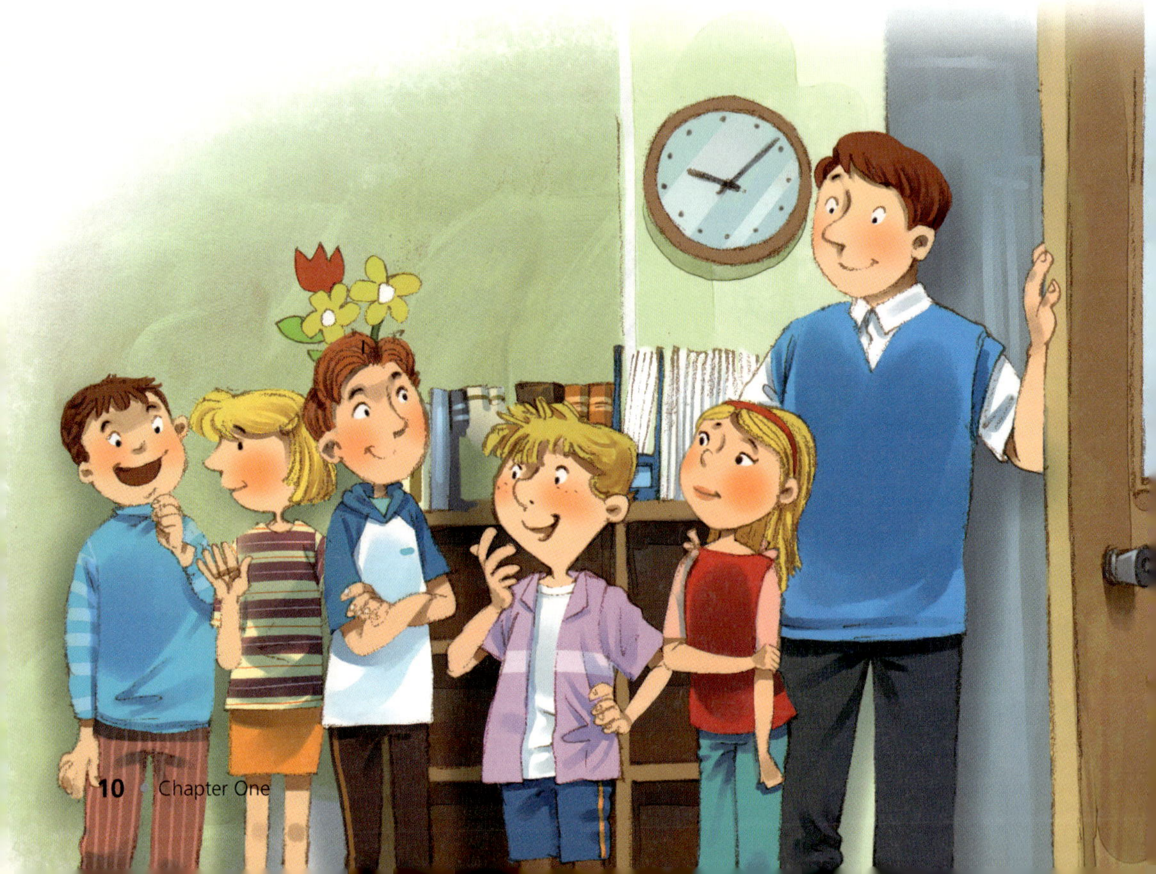

It was the 4th graders' turn to visit that afternoon.

"I wonder if there will be any sports stars there," whispered John.

Kyle whispered back, "Or famous celebrities."

"It's time to go," said their teacher, Mr. Harrison.

"But first, let's review a few instructions."

The students lined up at their classroom door and waited quietly.

KEY WORDS

- ghost
- squirm
- can't wait to
- grade
- gallery

- come alive
- grader
- turn
- wonder if
- whisper

- celebrity
- review
- instruction
- line up

Mr. Harrison began. "You will not have time to see every..."

"Ghost!" said John.

The class laughed.

"That's right," said Mr. Harrison.

"The 8th grade students will look very different today.
They are dressed up like famous people from all walks
of life.
But don't expect to meet someone famous from the
present.
These are famous people from the past. That's why they
are ghosts!"
"Ghosts are a little scary," said a girl named Claire at the
front of the line. She was a new student in their class.
"Don't worry," said Mr. Harrison.
"They won't scare you. They've worked hard to make
their presentations fun.
And you'll be surprised how much you learn."

KEY WORDS

- be dressed up
- all walks of life
- expect
- present
- past
- scary
- scare
- presentation

"I never expected to learn anything from a ghost," said Kyle.

"Me, neither," said John, smiling.

"Each of you may choose three ghosts to visit," said Mr. Harrison.

"It might be a good idea to go with a friend.  So first, you'll have to decide which three ghosts you'd like to see.

You will find a list in the library with the names of each famous person.

There will be a map, too, so you will be able to find your ghost. Ready?" he asked.

"Ready!" answered the class.

POP QUIZ

How many ghosts can each student visit?

ⓐ three
ⓑ as many as they like

KEY WORDS

- each of
- choose
- decide
- list
- be able to

A Gallery of Ghosts

John and Kyle stood in the doorway of the library.

The large room didn't look like their library anymore.

There were lots of white sheets draped over the

bookshelves and the computer stations.

Costumed girls and boys were scattered around the

room, motionless.

"It looks like a haunted house," muttered the new girl,

Claire. "It's creepy, isn't it?"

Kyle and John shrugged. But then Kyle had an idea.

"Would you like to go with us?" he asked.

Claire nodded, relieved.

It wasn't so much the ghosts that scared her.

She just didn't want to walk around by herself.

KEY WORDS

- doorway
- sheet
- drape
- bookshelf
- computer station
- costumed
- scatter
- motionless
- haunted
- mutter
- creepy
- shrug
- relieved
- by oneself

▲ Wilma Rudolph

"Where shall we go first?" asked Kyle.

They stood in front of the list, reading names.

"I love sports, especially basketball," said John.

He wanted to be a professional basketball player when he grew up. "Are there any athletes on the list?"

"Wilma Rudolph, the Olympic track star, is there," said Claire. "I'll bet she played basketball."

"Let's start with her,"
said John. "Who's
next?"

"I like inventing
things," said Kyle.
Kyle was always
taking things apart,
but he could never put
them back together
again.

"Thomas Edison is
here. Can we visit
him?"

"Sure," said Claire. "I guess that leaves me."

▲ Thomas Edison

- professional
- grow up (grow-grew-grown)
- athlete
- track
- star

- I'll bet...
- invent
- take ... apart
- put ... back

▲ Hans Christian Andersen

She looked down the list and read the names. But she was having a hard time, making a choice.

"What do you like?" asked John.

"I like stories," said Claire quietly. A blush spread across her face. What Claire really loved was writing stories.

"Hans Christian Andersen is here," said Kyle.

"He wrote fairy tales, didn't he?"

"Fairy tales?" said John. "Yuck." He wasn't a big fan of
fairy tales.

But John noticed that Claire's face lit up at the mention
of Hans Christian Andersen.

She smiled brightly for the first time since they'd arrived
in the library.

"Alright," said John. "We'll go see Hans."

"Let's check the map now so we'll know where to find
our ghosts," said Kyle.

"Do you have to call them ghosts?" Claire frowned.

"Yes!" Kyle and John answered in unison.

They laughed out loud then, and Claire couldn't help
smiling, too.

KEY WORDS

- yuck
- big fan of
- notice
- light up (light-lit-lit)
- mention

- for the first time
- frown
- in unison
- out loud
- can't help + *Verb*-ing

A Who might say each line? Match each line with the person who is likely to say it.

❶ I'm curious about sports stars. •

• a) 

❷ I'm a 4th grade teacher. •

• b) 

❸ I don't want to walk around alone. •

• c) 

❹ I have an idea that will help another student. •

• d) 

B Circle the right word(s) for each underlined part.

❶ John and Kyle are students in the (8th / 4th) grade.

❷ The special program will be in the (cafeteria / library).

❸ The speakers are called "ghosts" because they are from the (present / past).

❹ John and Kyle (will / will not) have time to visit every ghost.

C Choose the best answer to each question.

❶ Why will the 8th graders look different?

a) They will be dressed like famous people.

b) They will be dressed as monsters.

c) They will all be wearing hats.

d) They will not be wearing shoes.

❷ Which of these instructions did Mr. Harrison NOT give?

a) The students may visit three ghosts.

b) The students might want to go with a friend.

c) The students will find a list in the library with the names of the famous people.

d) The students should ask questions.

D Mark T for true or F for false.

❶ John wonders if there will be sports stars in the library.　T　F

❷ John and Kyle are afraid to go in the library.　T　F

❸ The students believe that there are real ghosts in the library.　T　F

❹ The 8th graders will look like famous people from the past.　T　F

A Champion's Challenges

Kyle pointed to the right-hand corner of the room.

A tall African-American girl stood by an easel.

She was wearing white track shorts, a blue tank top, and running shoes.

She was frozen at her spot, like a statue.

On the easel next to her was a poster with black-and-white pictures.

In the center of the poster, in bold letters, was the name, "Wilma Glodean Rudolph."

There were two rows of chairs set up in front of the girl.

Claire, John, and Kyle sat down in the very front row.

KEY WORDS

- champion
- challenge
- point to
- right-hand
- corner
- African-American
- easel
- track shorts
- tank top
- running shoes
- frozen
- spot
- statue
- black-and-white
- center
- in bold letters
- row
- set up
- very

USA
Wilma Glodean Rudolph

A bell rang, and suddenly, all around the library, the frozen statues came to life!

"Hello," said the student.

"My name is Wilma Glodean Rudolph. I have also been called *The Black Gazelle*, *Skeeter*, and *The Tornado*."

John raised his hand. "What's a *Skeeter*?"

The student smiled.

"It's what we call a mosquito where I come from. Can you guess how I got all those nicknames?"

John nodded. "Because you're so fast!"

"Yes," she said. "I was an Olympic medalist in track and field!"

"Wow," whispered John.

She smiled and continued. "People called me the fastest woman on earth. But I didn't start out fast.

In fact, I struggled to overcome many handicaps when I was young."

John leaned forward in his seat.

He was even more interested now.

He had been struggling with his own problems on the basketball team.

KEY WORDS

- **ring** (ring-rang-rung)
- **come to life**
- **gazelle**
- **skeeter**
- **tornado**
- **mosquito**
- **nickname**
- **medalist**
- **track and field**
- **start out**
- **in fact**
- **struggle to**
- **overcome**
- **handicap**
- **lean forward**

He was one of the shortest players, and often sat on the bench. Wilma Rudolph might have a solution for him.

"I was born on June 23rd, 1940 and I was premature, which means I was born too early.

I only weighed four and a half pounds! When I was four, I contracted polio.

Though I survived the virus, I had to wear a clunky brace on my left leg and foot.

For five long years, I wore the brace and went to physical therapy for leg strengthening exercises.

The exercises were painful, and I had to work hard every day.

Even when the brace came off, I still had to wear an orthopedic shoe. My left foot was crooked and needed straightening.

Finally, after two more years, I was able to leave the special shoe behind forever."

John raised his hand. "You mean you couldn't run for all those years?"

"That's right," she said. "I was nearly twelve years old before I could move like other kids." She smiled.

KEY WORDS

- solution
- premature
- weigh
- pound
- contract polio
- survive
- virus
- clunky
- brace
- physical therapy
- strengthen
- painful
- come off
- orthopedic shoe
- crooked
- straighten
- leave ... behind
- forever
- nearly

"But I couldn't wait to catch up! When I saw my older sister playing basketball, I knew that was the sport for me.

It was great practice for running, so I played basketball as much as I could."

Claire nudged John, to make sure he was listening.

But John was hanging on every word.

He couldn't believe that Wilma Rudolph had gone from standing in a brace to standing on a podium, winning medals! How did she do it?

KEY WORDS

- catch up
- as much as I can
- nudge
- make sure

- hang on every word
- podium
- attend
- career

"I attended Burt High School and played on the
basketball team.
I worked hard, and quickly became one of the star
players.
During one of our games, Ed Temple, the Tennessee
State University track coach, saw me.
And that was the day that changed my sports career."

John couldn't wait to hear what Wilma Rudolph would say next!

"Coach Temple allowed me to train with the Tennessee State track team.

While I was still in high school, I qualified for the 1956 Olympics.

I went to Melbourne, Australia, and won a bronze medal.

After I graduated from high school, I attended Tennessee State University and worked even harder.

I wanted to win a gold medal when the 1960 Olympics were held in Rome, Italy."

She paused.

John was on the edge of his seat!  "Did you win a gold medal?"

> ## POP QUIZ
>
> Rudolph won a bronze medal in the Melbourne Olympics. Where is Melbourne?
>
> ⓐ England
> ⓑ Australia

KEY WORDS

- train
- qualify for
- bronze medal
- graduate from
- be held
- pause
- on the edge of one's seat (*cf.* edge)

"I won my gold medal," she said. Then she smiled from
ear to ear.

"I won three gold medals! I broke records for the
100-meter dash, and the 200-meter dash, too.
We broke a team record when we won the 4-by-100
meter relay.
It was a very exciting time for us. I was the first
American woman to win three gold medals in a single
Olympics!"

John tried not to be disappointed.

He had been hoping to learn Wilma Rudolph's secret to success.

But so far, all he'd learned was to work hard.

He worked hard every day, but he still spent most of his time on the bench.

KEY WORDS

- smile from ear to ear
- break a record
  (break-broke-broken)
- dash
- 4-by-100 meter relay
- single
- be disappointed
- secret
- so far
- spend (spend-spent-spent)
- most of

USA
Wilma
Glodean
Rudolph

"But here is what I want you to remember today," she
said. 📖 "Winning is great, sure, but if you are really
going to do something with your life, the secret is
learning how to lose."

John scratched his head.

Here at last was the secret to success.

But was Wilma Rudolph telling him to… lose?

"Nobody goes undefeated all the time," she continued.
"If you can pick up after a crushing defeat, and go on to
win again, you are going to be a champion someday."

KEY WORDS

- scratch
- at last
- undefeated
- pick up

- crushing defeat
- go on
- someday

The bell rang again and all the talking stopped.

The speakers froze and the younger students clapped.

But John was sitting as still as the statue-like speakers.

He was thinking about basketball, and the secret to
success that he'd learned.

He would not be defeated, sitting on the bench at the
basketball games.

He'd wait for his opportunity to play, and then give it his best shot.

Wilma Rudolph had waited seven years before she had her chance, and look where she had ended up!

Kyle and Claire were heading toward the other side of the library.

They were looking for a ghost holding a light bulb.

"Hey, wait up," called John. "What's the bright idea, leaving without me?"

KEY WORDS

- speaker
- **freeze** (freeze-froze-frozen)
- clap
- still
- statue-like
- defeated

- opportunity
- give it one's best shot
- end up
- head
- light bulb
- wait up

Chapter Two

Comprehension Quiz

A Mark T for true or F for false.

❶ John was impressed by Wilma Rudolph's speech.　T　F

❷ Wilma Rudolph was an Olympic medallist in tennis.　T　F

❸ People called Rudolph the fastest woman on earth.　T　F

❹ Wilma Rudolph was born fast.　T　F

B Put the sentences in order.

❶ Wilma could walk without a brace or special shoe.

❷ Wilma won three gold medals in Olympic game.

❸ Wilma contracted polio.

❹ While in high school, Wilma played on the basketball team.

❺ Wilma had to wear a clunky brace on her left leg and foot.

_______ → _______ → _______ → _______ → _______

Solve the crossword puzzle.

Across

❸ You are going to be a c________ someday.

❹ C________ Temple allowed Wilma to train with the track team.

❻ Wilma wanted to win a g________ medal.

❼ Wilma had to wear an o________ shoe.

❽ When Wilma was four, she contracted p________ .

Down

❶ Wilma played b________ as much as she could.

❷ Wilma struggled to overcome many h________ .

❺ Wilma went to physical t________ for leg strengthening exercises.

A Genius at Work

Kyle took his front row seat. "Sh!" he said.

Claire sat still, but John mumbled under his breath.

"He hasn't said anything yet."

"He will," said Kyle. "And I don't want to miss anything!"

The speaker was dressed in a three-piece business suit.

The chain of a pocket watch dangled across his chest.

In his right hand, he held a light bulb.

It was one of the old, incandescent types of bulb.

Behind him, a poster displayed dozens of inventions.

Kyle was counting them when the bell rang.

"Good afternoon," said the speaker.

"Allow me to introduce myself to you fine, young people.

I'm Thomas Alva Edison."

He tipped his head, then held up the light bulb.

KEY WORDS

- genius
- at work
- mumble under one's breath
- miss
- three-piece business suit
- chain
- pocket watch
- dangle
- incandescent
- display
- dozens of
- invention
- introduce
- tip

▲ light bulb

"You've probably heard about my little invention here."

He screwed the light bulb into a nearby lamp and turned it on.

"Ah, that's better. Now I can read my list of inventions."

He picked up a piece of paper.

"The light bulb, the phonograph, even alkaline storage batteries... Why, I have patents for over a thousand inventions!"

"A thousand!" said Kyle. "You own the rights to all those inventions?"

KEY WORDS

- screw
- nearby
- turn on
- phonograph
- alkaline storage battery
- why
- patent
- own

- right
- cup a hand
- deaf
- speak up
- scarlet fever
- addled
- old-fashioned
- confused

"What's that, you say?" The speaker cupped a hand
around his ear.

"I'm nearly deaf, so you'll have to speak up. I had
scarlet fever when I was four.

But I like questions. When I was seven and a student
like you, I asked so many questions, the teacher
called me 'addled.' That's an old-fashioned word for
'confused.'"

Edison smiled. "My mother was so angry, she kept me home, and taught me herself."

Kyle was surprised. Thomas Edison was called "addled"? Boy, was that teacher ever wrong. Everybody knows that Thomas Edison was a genius!

"I never went back to school. I started working, and coming up with new ideas, when I was a young boy. At 12 years old, I sold newspapers to passengers on the Grand Trunk Railroad line.

I did so well, I decided to write my own newspaper. I called it *The Grand Trunk Herald*. It sold pretty well, too.

But even at 12, I was busy with my experiments.
I'd set up a small laboratory in the train's baggage car.
Unfortunately, I made a mistake mixing chemicals and
the car caught fire."

A few students laughed. Kyle didn't think they should laugh.

Everybody makes mistakes once in a while.

Just yesterday, Kyle had tried to fix the toaster for his mother.

It was easy to take it apart, but he made a mess, trying to put it together again.

His mistake nearly caught fire, too!

Mr. Edison laughed. "Well, I didn't think it was funny at the time. I got kicked off the train and had to sell my papers in the stations.

But one day while I was working, I saved a small child who ran out in front of a train.

The child's father was so grateful, he taught me how to operate a telegraph. *Aha!* And that was the beginning of a new career for me.

So it was a good thing I got kicked off the train, wasn't it?"

He'd made a mistake, thought Kyle.

But Thomas Edison hadn't let a mistake stop him from what he loved to do.

▲ hand sending a telegraph message

- once in a while
- fix
- toaster
- make a mess
- kick off
- station
- grateful
- operate
- telegraph

"I enjoyed success as a telegrapher, but my deafness couldn't keep up with the changes.

Once the Morse Code messages were sent through a sounding board, I started having trouble. 

So I moved to Louisville, Kentucky and worked for Western Union.

I liked to work nights, when I could have the place to myself.

But one night, while working on an experiment, I spilled sulphuric acid on the floor.

It seeped down and landed on my boss's desk. I got fired from that job, too."

POP QUIZ

Where did Edison set up his first laboratory?

ⓐ New Jersey
ⓑ New York

KEY WORDS

- telegrapher
- deafness
- keep up with
- once
- Morse Code

- sounding board
- to oneself
- spill
- sulphuric acid
- seep

- land
- get fired
- awful
- by the time
- not long after

"Oh, no," said Kyle. "That must've been awful!"

"Well, young man, it was a difficult time for me. But I picked myself up and kept working on my inventions. And by the time I moved to New York, I sold one of those inventions for a lot of money.

Not long after that, I set up my first laboratory in New Jersey."

Kyle pointed to a picture on the poster.

Men in white coats were working at lab desks.

"Is that your laboratory?"

He smiled. "That's my big laboratory! I had scientists working alongside machinists there in Menlo Park, New Jersey.

And eventually, we developed the phonograph. Do you know what a phonograph is?"

Kyle raised his hand. "I do! It's like a record player."

"That's right, young man. I couldn't hear very well, but that didn't stop me from my experiments with sound. It was 1877 and I became famous all over the world after the phonograph was introduced. They called me 'The Wizard of Menlo Park.'"

▲ phonograph

What was the invention that made Edison famous around the world?

ⓐ the phonograph
ⓑ the telegraph

KEY WORDS

- **lab** (= laboratory)
- **alongside**
- **machinist**
- **eventually**
- **develop**
- **record player**
- **introduce**
- **wizard**

Kyle wished someone would call him a wizard. But he made a lot of mistakes. He wasn't sure he'd ever get it right.

"And you know the rest of the story," said Mr. Edison. "I became one of the most famous inventors and businessmen in America!"

He pointed to the lamp and smiled.

"I worked hard all my life, almost till the day I died. You've probably heard one of my favorite quotes: Genius is one percent inspiration and ninety-nine percent perspiration!"

KEY WORDS

- get it right
- rest
- businessman
- quote
- inspiration

- perspiration
- burst into applause (burst-burst-burst)
- clap
- sweat
- on one's way to

The students burst into applause as the bell rang,
freezing Thomas Edison.
Kyle clapped louder than anyone else.
He was thinking about all the times he'd sweated over
his work. He was on his way to being a genius!

Comprehension Quiz

A  Choose the best answer to each question.

❶ Why did Edison's mother keep her son from returning to school?

a) She needed help at home.

b) She didn't think he needed any more formal education.

c) She was angry with a teacher for calling her son "addled."

d) She was angry with a teacher who had punished her son.

❷ Which of the following statements is NOT true?

a) Edison wanted to give up after being fired the second time.

b) Edison moved to New York.

c) Edison continued to work hard.

d) Edison sold one of his inventions for a lot of money.

B Put the sentences in order.

❶ The child's father taught Edison how to use the telegraph.

❷ Edison was kicked off the train.

❸ Edison became a successful telegraph operator.

❹ Edison saved a child's life in the train station.

_______ → _______ → _______ → _______

Solve the crossword puzzle.

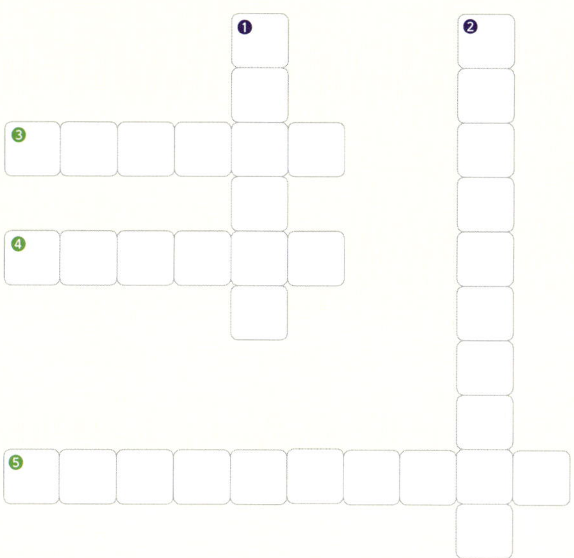

Across

❸ to create a process or device

❹ to say something quietly

❺ a room or building for experiments

Down

❶ to hang or swing loosely

❷ travelers on a train or a plane

invent	laboratory
dangle	mumble	passengers

Ugly Duckling

"Only one ghost left," said John.

"Hurry," said Claire. "Hans Christian Andersen is on the other side of the library."

"I don't see him," said Kyle.

"He's sitting in a chair," said Claire. "Behind all those books!"

Claire was right.

The ghost of Hans Christian Andersen was sitting at a desk, surrounded by books.

He was hunched over a paper, a quill pen frozen in his hand.

The students scrambled to take a seat. When the bell rang, the ghosts began their lively talks.

But the storyteller sat, head down, scribbling on the page.

KEY WORDS

- duckling
- other side
- surrounded by
- hunch
- quill
- scramble
- lively
- storyteller
- scribble

"Excuse me," said Claire. "Mr. Andersen?"

Claire hated to interrupt the famous author.

She knew how pleasant it was to get lost in writing.

For Claire, it was easier playing with made-up characters
than trying to make new friends.

He poked his head up and looked around. "Oh! I'm
sorry, children," he said. "Let me just finish this
sentence." Aha!

He wrote a word, and then smiled. "So, you would like
to hear a fairy tale?"

Claire would love to hear a fairy tale.

But she saw John make a face. Mr. Andersen must have seen John's face, too.

The storyteller stood up. "Well, I suppose I can tell you a little about myself, instead."

The students smiled.

"I was born in Odense, Denmark." He pointed to a spot
on the map.

"My mother was a washerwoman, and my father was a
shoemaker. But still, we were very poor.

The situation became worse when I was only eleven and
my dear father died.

I went to work in a tailor's shop, but I did not want to
be a tailor. I loved the theater. I loved to sing and dance.
I wanted to be a famous actor! I could not stay in
Odense where the people did not take me seriously. So I
left home."

Claire's heart was breaking, hearing his story.

She thought of the little ugly duckling in one of his fairy
tales.

The duckling had left home, too.

KEY WORDS

- spot
- washerwoman
- shoemaker
- situation
- worse

- dear
- tailor's shop
- tailor
- theater
- take ... seriously

"At fourteen, I went to the capital city of Copenhagen.
I had patrons, people who paid for my lessons in the
arts. But I failed miserably."

Discouraged again, thought Claire. Just like the ugly
duckling had been.

What would he do next, she wondered.

"A patron sent me to a school to get a proper education.
I was 17 years old then, five or six years older than most
of the students. The other students never accepted me.

KEY WORDS

- capital city
- patron
- miserably
- discouraged
- proper
- education

- accept
- headmaster
- sensitive
- cruel
- formal (↔ informal)
- Danish

The headmaster thought I was too sensitive, and was often cruel to me.

I left that school without learning to read or write formal Danish. I had failed yet again."

The old storyteller paused, as if he were remembering the pain and sadness of those days.

"But I did not give up! I completed my education and began to write.

For ten years, I wrote for adults. I penned stories, a play, and a book of poetry.

My work paid off when I was awarded a grant from the king himself and traveled across Europe."

Claire smiled. Despite failing over and over again, he kept trying. He was finally rewarded for his hard work!

KEY WORDS

- as if
- give up
- complete
- adult
- pen
- play
- poetry
- pay off
- award
- grant
- despite
- over and over again
- reward
- hard work

But Hans Christian Andersen was not famous for poetry or plays.

When had he written his fairy tales? When had he become the beautiful swan, the beloved storyteller?

He looked at Claire, and she felt as if he could read her mind.

"But you are wondering about the fairy tales, yes?

I wrote the first stories when I was thirty. But they were not so popular.

And then, in 1845, four publications came out, including *Wonderful Stories for Children*. Suddenly, I was famous! My tales became classics, read by children all over the world."

POP QUIZ

What was the publication for which Hans Christian
Andersen was famous?

ⓐ Wonderful Stories for Children
ⓑ Fairy Tales From Hans Christian Andersen

It had taken many years for Hans Christian Andersen to grow from an ugly duckling to a swan, but he had never given up.

He had moved from school to school before he found success.

Claire had moved often, too. But maybe in this school, she would try harder to make new friends.

Claire thought of what her mother always said: "If at first you don't succeed, try, try again."

"Life itself is the most wonderful fairy tale," said Hans Christian Andersen. **Aha!**

He picked up his pen.

The bell rang and Mr. Harrison called out to the class, "Line up! It's time to go!"

KEY WORDS

- find success
- at first
- itself
- call out
- take a look at

Claire started to leave, then turned to take one last look at Hans Christian Andersen.

She thought she heard him say, "Keep working on your stories!"

Claire caught up with Kyle. "Hey! Did you hear that?"

Kyle shook his head. "I didn't hear anything."

"Me, neither," said John. "You're just imagining things."

Claire smiled. Maybe she had imagined Hans Christian Andersen's encouraging words.

But imagined or not, she would continue to tell her own stories.

She'd put her active imagination to work as soon as she got home.

She'd write a story about the 8th graders' program. And she hoped Kyle and John would like to read it.

The speakers all around her were frozen, and the library was eerily quiet.

But Claire stopped long enough to wave her thanks.

She'd learned quite a bit from a gallery of ghosts!

KEY WORDS

- catch up with
- imagine
- encouraging
- put ... to work
- active

- imagination
- eerily
- wave one's thanks
- quite a bit

Why did Claire wave her hand when she left the library?

ⓐ She was trying to stop Kyle and John from leaving her behind.
ⓑ She wanted to thank the gallery of ghosts.

Comprehension Quiz

A  Match each person with the right description.

❶ Andersen's mother ·

❷ Hans Christian Andersen ·

❸ Andersen's father ·

· a) washerwoman

· b) died when Hans was eleven

· c) worked as a tailor

· d) shoemaker

B Mark T for true or F for false.

❶ Andersen was very successful in the theater. T F

❷ A patron refused to send Andersen to school for a proper education. T F

❸ Andersen's headmaster was often cruel to him. T F

❹ Many of the students in his school were eleven years old. T F

C Choose the best answer to each question.

❶ What did Hans Christian Andersen do when the bell rang in the library?

a) He left the library.   b) He continued to write.

c) He stayed frozen in place.   d) He read a book.

❷ Why did Andersen believe that his years of work paid off?

a) He became famous as a playwright.

b) A patron offered to send him on travels through Europe.

c) His work was published all over the world.

d) The king awarded him a grant.

D Fill in each blank with the right word below.

completed	accepted	rewarded	poked

❶ He _____________ his head up and looked around.

❷ The other students never _____________ me.

❸ I _____________ my education and began to write.

❹ He was finally _____________ for his hard work!

Let's Review the Story

Fill in the blanks to review the story.

❶ Title: ______________________

❷ Main Characters and Their Problems:

1. J __________ is short, and often sits on the b __________ during the b __________ games.

2. K __________ likes taking things apart, but often makes a m __________ putting them back together.

3. C __________ likes to w __________ but she is too shy to share her stories with anyone. She has trouble making f __________ .

❸ The Ghosts and Their Obstacles:

1. W __________ R __________ had p __________ in her leg and a crooked f __________ .

2. T __________ E __________ had n __________ formal s __________ , and was f __________ from jobs.

3. H __________ C __________ A __________ was p __________ and l __________ as a child. He f __________ often in s __________ .

❹ What Students Learned from the Ghosts:

1. W __________ R __________ won three Olympic g __________ medals in track and field, even though she couldn't r __________ like other kids until she was nearly t __________ !

2. T __________ E __________ made many m __________ , but he w __________ hard and never gave up on his i __________ .

3. A __________ struggled for many years before he wrote the f __________ t __________ that children still read today.

Let's Think & Talk

Think about the following questions and answer them freely.

❶ Wilma Rudolph experienced a great difficulty in her childhood, but she eventually overcame it and won three gold medals in the Olympics. What difficulty did she go through and how did she overcome it?

❷ Edison went through many crises when he was growing up, but he overcame them and created thousands of inventions. His inventions brought huge changes to human life. What crises did he go through and how did he overcome them?

❸ Andersen went through several crises when he was growing up, but he finally overcame them and became a children's storywriter whose stories continue to be loved by people. What crises did he go through and how did he overcome them?

❹ What crisis or difficulty are you going through? How will you overcome the crisis or difficulty and what kind of person do you want to be? Share your thoughts with friends.

❺ What great person do you want to meet? Tell us the reason why you want to meet him or her.

Let's Review the Story

❶ Title: A Gallery of Ghosts

❷ Main Characters and Their Problems:

1. John is short, and often sits on the bench during the basketball games.

2. Kyle likes taking things apart, but often makes a mess putting them back together.

3. Claire likes to write but she is too shy to share her stories with anyone. She has trouble making friends.

❸ The Ghosts and Their Obstacles:

1. Wilma Rudolph had polio in her leg and a crooked foot.

2. Thomas Edison had no formal schooling, and was fired from jobs.

3. Hans Christian Andersen was poor and lonely as a child. He failed often in school.

❹ What Students Learned from the Ghosts:

1. Wilma Rudolph won three Olympic gold medals in track and field, even though she couldn't run like other kids until she was nearly twelve!

2. Thomas Edison made many mistakes, but he worked hard and never gave up on his ideas.

3. Andersen struggled for many years before he wrote the fairy tales that children still read today.

After-reading Test

- A Gallery of Ghosts
- Level 4
- 28 Questions

  (Vocabulary 6 / Reading Comprehension 16 /

  Sentence Structure & Grammar 6)

1. What does "gallery" mean in the following sentence?

   > A Gallery of Ghosts: History Comes Alive!

   ① an outdoor balcony
   ② a room or building for the display
   ③ a room for studying
   ④ a large container

2. What does "track" mean in the following sentence?

   > Wilma Rudolph, the Olympic track star, is there.

   ① a line of rails on a railroad
   ② a footprint of an animal
   ③ sports that involve a running course
   ④ cars racing around a path

3. What does "premature" mean in the following sentence?

   > I was born on June 23rd, 1940 and I was premature.

   ① born looking old
   ② born too early
   ③ born without hair
   ④ born with weak legs

4. What does a "patent" mean in the following sentence?

   > Why, I have patents for over a thousand inventions!

   ① a picture of an invention
   ② a container for an invention
   ③ a right granted to an inventor to sell an invention
   ④ a person who helps an inventor

※ Choose the right word for each blank. (5~6)

5.

> I had ____________, people who paid for my lessons in the arts.

① servants
② patrons
③ coaches
④ headmasters

6.

> Edison believed that genius was one percent ____________ and
> ninety-nine percent ____________.

① inspiration, determination
② perspiration, education
③ inspiration, perspiration
④ dedication, determination

7. What will be surprising for the students attending the program?
① how much they will learn from ghosts
② how funny the ghosts will act
③ how scary the ghosts will be
④ how difficult it will be to visit the ghosts

8. Each student is allowed to visit three ghosts. Why does Mr. Harrison give
this instruction?
① There are only three ghosts in the library.
② The students will only have time to hear three presentations.
③ It is too difficult to find more than three ghosts.
④ Mr. Harrison likes the number "three."

9. Why did Kyle choose Thomas Edison?
① because he likes inventing things
② because he likes breaking things
③ because he likes drawing pictures
④ because he likes dreaming about electricity

10. John guesses that Wilma Rudolph is fast based on her nicknames. Why?
   ① The ghost explains the nicknames.
   ② All of the names describe something that is speedy.
   ③ John is a lucky guesser.
   ④ All of the names are about track and field sports.

11. What sport is causing problems for John?
   ① soccer   ② baseball
   ③ track   ④ basketball

12. What did Rudolph need after she survived polio?
   ① bandage on her leg   ② cast on her leg
   ③ brace on her leg   ④ patch on her leg

13. Rudolph won three gold medals in the Olympics. Where were they held?
   ① Rome, Italy
   ② Milan, Italy
   ③ Montreal, Canada
   ④ Mexico City, Mexico

14. John listens to Wilma Rudolph's story and knows that he will ___________.
   ① continue to sit on the bench and boo the other players
   ② wait patiently for his chance and then take his best shot
   ③ quit basketball and try another sport
   ④ never be a very good basketball player

15. Which description fits the ghost of Thomas Edison?

① a three piece suit and hat

② a three piece suit and pocket watch

③ a two piece suit and boots

④ a lab coat and glasses

16. Which three inventions does Thomas Edison list?

① the telegraph, the light bulb, the camera

② the alkaline batteries, the radio, the phonograph

③ the light bulb, the phonograph, the ball point pen

④ the light bulb, alkaline batteries, the phonograph

17. What caused Thomas Edison's deafness?

① a blow to the head when he was four

② scarlet fever when he was four

③ an ear infection when he was four

④ an unknown illness when he was four

18. Kyle doesn't think the other students should laugh at Edison's story about the fire. Why?

① A fire is not a laughing matter.

② The students are being disrespectful.

③ Everybody makes mistakes once in a while.

④ The fire story is not true.

19. Why did Edison have a problem with the telegraph?

① He could not keep up with the dots and dashes of the Morse Code.

② He was quickly bored with the telegraph.

③ He broke his telegraph equipment.

④ He could not hear the Morse Code signals very well through the sounding board.

20. Why must Claire hurry to see the last ghost?
  ① The library is about to close for the day.
  ② The ghost is walking out of the library.
  ③ The program is about to end.
  ④ The ghost is on the other side of the library.

21. Claire would prefer playing with made-up friends rather than ____________.
  ① completing her homework
  ② playing with John and Kyle
  ③ trying to make new friends
  ④ writing a new story

22. When Andersen's fairy tales were first published, they were ____________.
  ① not so popular
  ② enormously popular
  ③ miserable failures
  ④ loved by children all over the world

※ Choose the wrong part of each sentence. (23~24)

23.
When I saw my older sister played basketball, I knew that
    ①   ②   ③   ④
was the sport for me.

24.
Life itself is the wonderfulest fairy tale.
    ①   ②   ③   ④

25.
> They couldn't ＿＿＿＿＿＿ to go to their school's library!

① want ② need
③ wait ④ love

26.
> It might be a good idea ＿＿＿＿＿＿ go with a friend.

① for ② to
③ that ④ as

※ Choose the correct sentence. (27~28)

27. ① John tried to not be disappointed.
② John tried not to be disappointed.
③ John tried to be not disappointed.
④ John tried to be disappointed not.

28. ① But here is where I want you to remember today.
② But here is which I want you to remember today.
③ But here is what I want you to remember today.
④ But here is how I want you to remember today.

Cathy C. Hall

Cathy C. Hall graduated with a broadcasting degree, working in the radio industry as a news reporter and commercial copywriter before going back to school to earn English certification. She spent a decade in education, teaching preschoolers, middle schoolers, and high schoolers. Now, she's a full-time freelance writer, with stories, essays, and poems in publications for both children and adults. Her byline appears in books like *Uncle John's Facts To Annoy Your Teacher, Chicken Soup for the Soul's Think Positive for Kids, Cup of Comfort for Dog Lovers*, and many more. She lives near Atlanta, Georgia, with her husband and a miniature dachshund.

A Gallery of Ghosts

Written by Cathy C. Hall
Illustrated by Eungyeong Song

First Published in October 2015

Editorial Manager: Juyon Choi
Editors: Juyon Choi, Hyunjung Kim, Kyunghee Jang, Jiyeong Park
Designers: Eunhee Lee, Elim
Cover Designer: Eunhee Lee

Published and distributed by

Darakwon Bldg., 64-1 Jandari-ro, Mapo-gu, Seoul, Korea 04031
Tel: 82-2-736-2031(ext. 250)   Fax: 82-2-732-2037
Homepage: www.ihappyhouse.co.kr
Publisher: Kyudo Chung

ISBN: 978-89-6653-205-6 18740 / 978-89-6653-156-1 18740(set)

[Components]
• 1 Audio CD (Recording Studio: Aram)
• Answer Keys & Korean Translation: Free download at www.ihappyhouse.co.kr